LOVE CAN BE *Messy*

Relationship Tips for Couples and Singles

BUT YOU DON'T HAVE TO BE

ELIZABETH OVERSTREET

Copyright © 2024 by Elizabeth Overstreet

All rights reserved. This book may not be reproduced or stored in whole or in part by any means without the written permission of the author except for brief quotations for the purpose of review.

ISBN: 978-1-963569-38-4 (hard cover)
978-1-963569-39-1 (soft cover)

Edited by: Amy Ashby

Published by WARREN Publishing
Charlotte, NC
www.warrenpublishing.net
Printed in the United States

Learn more here how you can have an unmessy love life.

I dedicate this book to my parents, Alline and Samuel Overstreet, whose unwavering commitment serves as a living testament to the profound impact of building a lasting legacy of love. Their inspiring journey has helped me to shape a roadmap for individuals and couples to explore the transformative potential of crafting a resilient love story that can stand the test of time.

CONTENTS

INTRODUCTION 3

CHAPTER 1: Love—and Your Connection to It—Starts Early 19

CHAPTER 2: The Naked Truth About Self-Love: It's Not Just About Loving Yourself 25

CHAPTER 3: Forget the Fairy Tale: The Reality of What a Healthy Relationship Looks Like 35

CHAPTER 4: No One Is Perfect, Even You: Unlocking the Secrets to a Healthy and Rewarding Relationship 43

CHAPTER 5: The Healthy Relationship Road Map: How to Navigate Your Relationship Roadblocks 51

CHAPTER 6: The Power of Teamwork: The Common Factor for a Happy and Healthy Relationship 59

CONCLUSION 67

OTHER RELATIONSHIP BOOKS TO REFERENCE 69

ACKNOWLEDGMENTS 73

INTRODUCTION

I am an avid observer of relationships. I've been observing relationships—my own, as well as others—for decades. I know how to succeed at dating and building a healthy and rewarding relationship.

Here are the five basic rules for relationship success:

- The Naked Truth About Self-Love: It's Not Just About Loving Yourself
- Forget the Fairy Tale: The Reality of What a Healthy Relationship Looks Like
- No One Is Perfect, Even You: Unlocking the Secrets to a Healthy and Rewarding Relationship
- The Healthy Relationship Road Map: How to Navigate Your Relationship Roadblocks
- The Power of Teamwork in Healthy Relationships: The Common Factor for a Happy and Healthy Relationship

Our obsession with finding *the one* permeates our culture. From reality shows that paint the fairy tale of idyllic love, TV programs that always show major relationship issues happily solved within a one-hour window or less, and the relentless presence of social media depicting the perfect couple, we are bombarded by the idea that there is *one* person out there for each of us. Supposedly, once we find this *one* person, all of our relationship challenges will be put to rest. Society creates an unrealistic picture of what love looks like and how healthy and rewarding relationships are built. It's easy to be fooled into thinking that love and having a relationship are easy. However, the truth is that having a healthy and loving relationship takes some work.

In listening to my family, friends, and loved ones go through the ups and downs of their relationships, I've learned what works and what doesn't. For example, with family members I've observed in long-term relationships, I've noticed how "bigger decisions"—like planning events, looking over finances, and determining what is in the family's best interest—work when there is collaboration and input from both people in the relationship. In relationships I've observed that have lasted for multiple decades, there have been times of great joy and happiness. However, there have also been times of incredible difficulty and challenges. These couples are able to navigate these challenges because they've built healthy practices into their relationships, which has helped them during the difficult times.

No relationship is perfect. However, most of us want to be in a relationship that is happy, healthy, and rewarding. When you have the right tools and understanding of what it takes to build a healthy relationship, it can be the difference between a relationship that is short lived or one that is long lasting. Being equipped with knowledge of what a healthy relationship looks like allows you to enter into a new relationship with your eyes wide open. You can then start things off with realistic expectations and a road map of how to navigate those touchy areas or difficult moments that often will surface.

At the beginning of a relationship, it's often easy to overlook certain things that may not be as bothersome about the other person. This stage is often referred to as the "honeymoon phase." During this time your dopamine receptors and oxytocin levels—the brain chemicals that make you feel good—are higher than normal. Oxytocin is a hormone produced in the brain that is often called the "love drug" or "love hormone."

Because of these chemical releases, couples who have recently fallen in love often have an extra dose of emotions that help them overcome the early challenges they may face in a relationship. It's easy, while on this high, for negative things you would normally notice about someone to be diminished. The honeymoon phase can last up to two years on average, which also explains how sometimes, even when a couple has been together for a while, one partner might remark that they feel like they don't really know the other. Those feel-good emotions they experienced at the onset of the relationship may have limited their ability to see their partner fully.

Later, when a person reflects back following the honeymoon period of the relationship, they are often able to pinpoint that moment in time when they knew something might have been amiss in the relationship. After those feel-good emotions have passed and the honeymoon phase has worn off, they can now clearly see more facets of their partner, including the desirable and not-so-desirable traits they possess.

Therefore, when two people come together and decide they want to be in a long-term relationship with each other, it's important that they talk things out, plan together, and lean into each other in areas where one individual may have a stronger skill set or more experience. When couples communicate, collaborate, and learn to let each other take the lead in areas in which each person excels, it enriches their relationship overall. Discord, on the other hand, occurs when there isn't communication between the two individuals, assumptions are made about the other person, one person goes ahead and makes a decision without the input of the other, or couples still operate as if they're single versus being in a relationship. This improper communication and lack of collaboration creates friction and disconnect.

One couple I coached, Jacob and Michelle, made an agreement that when either of them made any large purchases over $500, they would discuss it with each other first before moving forward with the purchase. However, Michelle would repeatedly go and make purchases over $500 without talking to Jacob about it beforehand. Because they had made an agreement to discuss these purchases, her covert purchasing created friction and discord in their relationship. When one person in a relationship doesn't honor agreed-upon commitments, these actions can cause tension to such a degree that it can in turn cause a breakdown of trust and partnership. While it might seem minor to the person breaking the agreement, this type of behavior, especially if repeated, can severely fragment the relationship and eventually cause irreparable damage.

Some couples may find themselves feeling disconnected from each other because they have been making assumptions about their partner's expectations instead of having a conversation and holding each other accountable. This kind of assumption can happen both knowingly and unknowingly. If you've been experiencing this disconnection in your relationships, you have to give yourself some grace. The fact that you are reading this book shows you are aware that you have relationship blind spots. We all do! I will help you learn how to tackle them. Self-awareness is the first step to having a healthy and rewarding relationship.

Look, it's not your fault if you've struggled. Maybe you grew up in an environment where you didn't see healthy relationships modeled for you. Maybe you experienced some traumatic events in your life that left you wounded, hurt, and lost when it comes to relationships. You're not alone. At times we can all be too hard on ourselves. In fact, we are often hard on ourselves just for having specific feelings that are completely normal to have. Some of these feelings may include inadequacy, a lack of self-confidence, or an inability to allow yourself to be vulnerable or heard. These feelings may be attributed to how we experienced love from others, like our parents, or relationships that left us wounded. You may think your feelings are only your own, not shared by others. This is not true. We are all human. Each of us has both positive and challenging moments in our interactions with those we love.

When you are in a relationship, it's unrealistic to believe you won't have moments of frustration, anger, and irritation. However, when you observe other couples who don't appear to be experiencing the same, it's easy to get stuck on how your relationship measures up. Once you take the time to dig deeper, though, you will find that every couple experiences similar negative emotions, and how they express those emotions is often based on the modeling they have seen or learned in other relationships. Some may have learned that their mom or dad wouldn't express frustration with their partner directly, but instead vented more indirectly with family members or friends. Other times couples hide their anger and irritation, eventually reaching a boiling point where tensions become so high that those emotions are then expressed at inopportune times. And some may have expressed their emotions in extreme and inappropriate ways such as yelling, being emotionally or physically abusive, or completely shutting down from interacting with their significant other. These cues we have observed in relationships around us can lead to us not being fully aware of how to practice and create healthy relationship habits. However, physical and emotional abuse is unacceptable in a relationship. In case you find yourself stuck in one of these situations, I've included some recommended resources at the end of this introduction.

Ideally, we want to be able to share with our significant others what bothers us. But because of our awareness of each other's sensitivities, sharing our frustrations can be easier said than done. We often get trapped in our feelings as opposed to allowing ourselves to feel the way we need to feel. For example, sometimes we intuitively know that a relationship dynamic isn't working. However, we remain in that relationship even when we know it isn't the best for us. We may justify staying based on our desire for companionship or a fear of being lonely, or maybe we're scared we won't find the person who is right for us. We may not want to face starting over; it can feel overwhelming to end an unhealthy relationship. So sometimes we allow our feelings to override our logic and intuition.

I coach clients who are often at a point where they have decided to end their relationships. They can clearly identify the breaking point of their relationships, but oftentimes they have kept going anyway, ignoring those feelings, thoughts, and experiences until they can't ignore them anymore. For example, one couple I worked with loved each other a great deal. However, they had vastly different views on spirituality. For one of the individuals, spirituality was a driver that poured into other parts of their life. They practiced a particular religion. It impacted how they functioned in the community, how they were raising their kids, and how they lived their life. They attended religious services regularly and spent a lot of time with those in their religious community. The other person didn't see spirituality in the same way. They weren't a big believer in attending religious services and felt that spirituality should be more informally practiced versus tied to a specific religion. This couple had to make a decision to determine if they wanted to continue their relationship or if they could compromise. They were planning to blend families and possibly have children together in the future, but the glaring differences in their spiritual and religious preferences took a toll on the relationship over time. Each held strong beliefs on this issue, and they eventually decided to part ways, even though they had repeatedly tried to work through these issues. They had

> WHEN YOU COMPARE YOURSELF TO OTHERS, YOU LOSE OUT ON THE RELATIONSHIP DYNAMIC THAT WORKS BEST FOR YOU.

each known and felt all along that they weren't aligned and were aware of the impact and confusion these differences could create in their family dynamic if they moved forward. Still, they kept trying to hang in there despite their obvious differences until it became apparent they couldn't reach a consensus.

Another factor that can affect whether a couple decides to stay together is feeling that their relationship should mimic someone else's. Due to generally accepted perceptions of how a relationship should be, we often compare ourselves to others. I've been there. You have too. We compare our situations to a friend's; we look to relationships we perceive to be what we *want* instead of exploring what we *need* to be happy with ourselves and our partners. When you compare yourself to others, you lose out on the relationship dynamic that works best for *you*. This unhealthy comparison can lead us to break up with someone because of how we feel others might perceive our relationship rather than choose the relationship dynamic that works best for us.

I have learned that the two biggest downfalls of a relationship are (1) comparing yourselves to others and (2) thinking of how your relationship "should" be versus understanding how a relationship evolves. The reality is a relationship is built over time and incrementally. Couples you may see ten, fifteen, or twenty years from now will look much different than they did when their relationship started. It's because these couples are continually building their relationships, discovering each other, and developing their understanding of each other. To build a relationship that is long-lasting, happy, and rewarding, a couple needs several elements. The analogy that comes to mind is the construction of a house. For a house to be able to withstand storms that comes its way, it needs to be built with a solid foundation. If a house is laid on a weak foundation, it is susceptible to ongoing issues via storms, defects in the structure of the house, etc.

REMEMBER: YOU ARE 50 PERCENT OF THE PROBLEM AND 100 PERCENT OF THE SOLUTION.

A strong foundation is also needed to build a healthy relationship. This foundation is made of several materials that start with each of you first, then extend between the two of you to form a healthy relationship. The first material for a strong foundation is self-accountability. If you cannot be self-accountable, you will leave your relationship exposed and vulnerable to collapsing. That is why so often in relationships where there is a lack of self-accountability, healthy love evades us. Self-accountability is your ability to honestly assess how you function in relationships, build awareness of your blind spots, and adapt in those areas that prevent you from connecting to healthy relationships. Remember: you are 50 percent of the problem and 100 percent of the solution.

In order to break the pattern of connecting to relationships that are unhealthy, it's important for us to understand who we are first. This knowledge is at the core of our foundation for a healthy relationship. If we are unsure of what our value is, what values are important to us, and the role we see a relationship playing in our life, it becomes easier for us to remain in relationships that do not serve us.

The second element for your relationship foundation is self-love. Self-love isn't just about loving yourself. Self-love provides clarity, vision, and an understanding of the value you bring to the relationship. Self-love is the North Star in your relationship, providing you with discernment to connect to healthy relationships and disconnect from unhealthy ones.

Finally, couples who are successful in maintaining happy and healthy relationships practice emotional intimacy. Emotional intimacy is one of the final components to your relationship. Ongoing maintenance is necessary to keep your home in good shape once it's constructed. Relationships require similar maintenance in the form of emotional intimacy. Emotional intimacy is being able to show up as who you are in a relationship. Without emotional intimacy, people shut down, creating barricades in the relationship. Instead of building together, couples may end up building separately. How we respond to our partners when they reveal themselves to us and how they react to us when we reveal ourselves can lead to more building or more separation in the relationship.

It can be difficult to be emotionally intimate. We may shut down or respond poorly due to the wired responses we carry as a result of our relationship experiences. We may have unresolved trauma related to unhealthy relationships we observed growing up. Or we may have conditioned ourselves to respond based on how others have responded to us when we have revealed our sacred emotions. That's why couples who build with each other need a team mindset to navigate the touchy topics or storms that can damage a relationship's foundation. Trusted advisors—such as a counselor, coach, pastor, or other couples who can mentor you, etc.—can help you continue to construct and strengthen your relationship. Just as a house has a blueprint that has been developed by a team of experts to ensure that its important components—plumbing, roof, foundation, etc.—remain intact, couples may need additional support to help them recognize and navigate aspects of their relationship that might be unclear or challenging. They may need additional support and should seek the appropriate guidance to help build and strengthen their relationships. Without developing and having emotional intimacy, it's difficult to build communication, trust, and respect for each other. This is also why many relationships end up faltering—just like a poorly constructed house.

Getting to know your significant other and falling in sync with them takes time. As I mentioned before, each relationship evolves and starts to look different as the relationship matures. For example, at the beginning of a relationship, we are often putting our best foot forward. That may mean, as a man, you have habits such as bringing your wife flowers unexpectedly or taking her out on dates. And as a woman, it may mean you are paying close attention to doing the things that your significant other adores about you, such as wearing that special outfit you know he likes or preparing that particular meal. It might mean spending time at sporting events together or participating in other activities you know he or she holds dear—like gaming. I'm using generic examples because each couple is different, but the bottom line is couples do things for each other out of love and appreciation. But as time passes and both people become more comfortable in a relationship, they may stop doing those things that helped to build emotional connections at the onset of the relationship. There can be several reasons for this. It could be because you have different responsibilities. It could be because you've lost interest in those parts of your relationship. However, as my wise grandmother would always say, "Don't start things you don't plan to continue."

Because relationships are built incrementally and day by day, it's so important to continue those little things that made your relationship special in the beginning. Courting your significant other in ways that are meaningful to them shouldn't stop once you are in a committed relationship. Romantic and loving gestures are constant reminders of the reasons you decided to be in a relationship in the first place. While these little acts of love may evolve as couples grow with each other, doing things you know your partner likes and appreciates should be continuous because this signals to them that you value and appreciate them. All of these efforts impact your relationship and your experiences with your partner. But it's the consistency of these habits that help you to build a healthy and strong relationship.

There is a lot of pressure placed on us by what we see on TV and social media, and we create myths based on what we *think* other people's relationships look like versus what they *actually* are in reality. All of these perceptions and limited observations can take you down the wrong path in your relationships.

Remember this: the only people who truly know what is happening in a relationship are the two people in that relationship! It's rare that others get to see the whole truth. This is why so many of our perceptions surrounding what a relationship should look like are dead wrong. So I don't know about you, but I'm so over relationship comparison. Comparison doesn't work!

SAY GOODBYE TO COMFORT, FAMILIARITY, AND EVERY OTHER EXCUSE FOR STAYING IN RELATIONSHIPS THAT SIMPLY AREN'T RIGHT.

I'm saying goodbye to comfort, familiarity, and every other excuse for staying in relationships that simply aren't right. Comfort and familiarity don't make my life happier or my relationships stronger. And if you've been in a relationship that was unfulfilling or unhealthy, I think you will agree! Maybe it's time to change the narrative of your story and how you see relationships. But in order to do that, you must first figure out who *you* are before you enter into another relationship for which you are not fully ready.

After going through a series of ups and downs in relationships, it's easy and tempting to want to give up, settle for less, or withdraw from relationships. It's easy to want to protect your heart after it has been broken or when you have felt blindsided by a relationship. And it can be hard to take the time to fully investigate your feelings and discover who you are before you begin dating again because often we are looking for others to fill in the gaps we feel we lack in ourselves. So you look externally for someone to complete you—until you face the hard truth that your completion has to come internally first and that being in a relationship will not make you whole. (I have a whole chapter dedicated to that one for you!) That's why self-reflection and self-awareness are so critical to establishing a solid foundation as you enter your next relationship.

That's what this book provides for you: a new way of looking at yourself so you can bring your best dating persona forward. That way you will be able to attract a partner who is the right one for you—or enhance your current relationship if you've already found the one.

I have been married before; I have gone through a divorce. I have had long-term relationships, and I have dated as a single parent. I am now remarried. All of these experiences taught me what I need in a relationship: I learned how to value myself before allowing someone else into my space. Since then, I have coached and mentored others who are married, divorced, cohabitating, single—and unhappy. I have discussed and advised, sharing perspectives on dating, love, marriage, and being happy within a relationship. It was only after I focused on building the foundation of my own relationships by starting with myself first and pulled together the observations of those multidecade relationships that were happy and healthy, that I was able to understand and connect the dots as to why healthy relationships often evade us and how we can achieve them.

Throughout my personal and professional observations, I have heard every fluffy theory that exists about relationships, and there's so much advice out there, it's hard to weed through what actually helps and what's a waste of time. My mission is to provide *practical* tools that help you discover your path to love. The process of finding someone and falling in love should not be a burdensome task. This book will start the dialogue and help you see that no matter who you are, there is someone who will love and accept you unconditionally.

Ready? Okay. Let's get you on the right path to relationship success.

> **DOMESTIC ABUSE SUPPORT SERVICES**
> If you are experiencing physical abuse and you need help, you can contact the National Domestic Violence Hotline. They provide confidential assistance and guidance to individuals facing abusive relationships. You can reach them at 1-800-799-SAFE (7233) in the United States.

Additional Resources:
- **The National Coalition Against Domestic Violence (NCADV):** NCDAV offers information, resources, and assistance for those affected by domestic violence. www.ncadv.org
- **Loveisrespect.org:** This resource is specifically designed for young people and provides information about healthy relationships, signs of abuse, and how to get help.
- **Rape, Abuse & Incest National Network (RAINN):** While RAINN focuses primarily on sexual violence, they also

provide valuable resources for those in abusive relationships. www.rainn.org
- **Local Support Services:** Search for local organizations or shelters that specialize in providing assistance to individuals experiencing abuse. They can often offer personalized help and safety planning.

Remember that your safety is the top priority. If you are in immediate danger, call emergency services in your country. It's important to reach out to professionals who can provide guidance tailored to your specific situation.

1

LOVE—AND YOUR CONNECTION TO IT—STARTS EARLY

The strong desire for us to connect with others is natural given that love starts so early in our lives. Think about it from a symbiotic perspective: you acquired this desire to love during the time you were in your mother's womb. Then, as you grew and developed into a fetus, you became physically connected to your mother in the closest way possible. You were acutely aware of her voice, heartbeat, and warmth. She, in essence, was your safety net.

Being delivered from the safety of a mother's body is perhaps one of the most traumatic events we all must experience. The transition from a safe, warm, and cozy environment into the real world is difficult. A mother is most needed by her baby during those early days to nurture and help her baby find their space in the world. However, as you develop into a child, you go through various phases as you learn to operate more independently while still having the reassurance of emotional connection with your mother. Some initial phases may be going from being breastfed to being fed by bottle to you holding your own bottle. Later phases may be learning to eat solids and learning how to walk, talk, and do other things on your own. Each period of your life from being an infant, toddler, child, tween, teen, and adult creates a different level of resilience in you and varying needs of emotional support from your mother or primary caregiver. And how your caregivers provided this emotional support now impacts how you approach your relationships with others.

As we continue to evolve into independent adults, we seek a connection with someone who understands and loves us for who we are. This transference of our love and attachment is normal and healthy, and it's the reason why there is often a very powerful connection when you meet someone, interact with them, and form a close relationship in which you realize they *get you* and *accept you* for who you are and what you are. This closeness is exactly what you've been looking for, because you're still searching for the kind of attachment you received growing up. Your attachment style can be even more complex if you lost a parent at a young age, experienced a tumultuous childhood, or were separated from your birth parents. This attachment is a normal part of who you are as a human, and it's what you have been wanting—possibly your whole life.

ATTACHMENT IS A NORMAL PART OF WHO YOU ARE AS A HUMAN, AND IT'S WHAT YOU HAVE BEEN WANTING —POSSIBLY YOUR WHOLE LIFE.

This connection to the right someone is so strong initially, it can make you dive in head first and go deep, expressing emotions you might not have known you had. As you go through these feelings—the rush and excitement in the beginning, the emotional connection that is built over time, the infatuation, attraction, and getting through difficult times—with your significant other and along with experiencing the struggles, ups and downs, and immense joys leads to you forming a bond of love and connection.

Love is both a wonderful and a scary thing. Allowing yourself to be vulnerable to another person is the ultimate connection in that you feel the safety net of someone who loves and values you, just like you felt in your mother's womb. Without this connection and feeling of safety, a relationship is doomed and cannot grow and flourish.

If you think of how you connected to your caregivers, this is the first example that shaped your emotions, opinions, and observations about love and relationships. The nature of your upbringing is often why relationships can be so complex. Finding a relationship that mimics your experience with your caregivers can give you mixed signals of what constitutes building a healthy relationship. Depending on how healthy your attachment was with your caregivers, your past experiences could send you looking for qualities your familial connection may have been lacking, qualities you were fortunate to have, or those areas in which you were maybe unhealthily attached. In other words, the way in which we form the foundation to our relationships is based on what we have observed in those relationships closest to us. But because all relationships are imperfect, it can be hard to pick out the key components needed to build a healthy relationship.

In some cases, your parents' or caregivers' behaviors might have had such a strong impact it can take a long time to identify the negative behaviors you were taught. So when you begin to feel comfortable with or fall in love with someone who isn't good for you, it's likely because the person demonstrates qualities and behaviors similar to your parents'—and you may not even realize how unhealthy that is!

Sometimes you get stuck doing things a certain way in your relationships based on what you have observed from your parents. As you build self-awareness, this may change, or if your relationships are tumultuous, you may learn to approach them differently. And while the way you are raised has a significant impact on who you are, it is not the only way in which your relationships are shaped. Through life experiences and relationships, your mindset can broaden, helping you to understand the value of the other components that build a healthy relationship. Approaching your relationship in a healthy manner requires self-awareness, recognition of the foundation created by how you grew up, and an understanding of how that foundation has impacted who you are as a person. Connecting the dots between these pieces can be crucial toward uncovering the blind spots that might prevent you from building a healthy relationship and can help you to recognize the attributes you already possess.

I know that finding love can be daunting. There is tremendous social pressure to be your best at all times when seeking love. This pressure has created an atmosphere in which everyone must constantly up their game, consider all their options, and keep up with the latest in relationship advice in order to find the best mate possible. However, too much flexing and bending can lead you away from the relationship you want. This "rule following" may lead you to look for unrealistic relationships or cause you to get involved in unhealthy relationships and settle for situations in which you are not truly happy.

Oftentimes when people find they are not connecting to the right person and there are recurring negative themes, there is a reason: they aren't showing up as themselves. Perhaps you are a people pleaser, and in your relationships, you constantly sacrifice your needs, wants, and feelings for the other person. You may try to appease the other person to the point where you hide who you are to make the relationship work. But when you do this, you are suppressing what you want and what you feel you deserve—and that *doesn't* work! Not being clear on who you are, what you bring to the table, and what you feel will complement your needs, desires, and wants keeps you in a relationship cycle of attracting people who are incompatible. It's time to break that cycle!

The first step of establishing clarity in your relationships with others is to establish clarity with *yourself*. I'll repeat that one. The first step toward establishing clarity in your relationships with others is to establish clarity with yourself. In all of the most fulfilling, satisfying, and long-lasting relationships I have either coached or observed, there is a theme: all of these individuals feel they can show up as themselves in their relationships—unabashedly.

> THE FIRST STEP TOWARD ESTABLISHING CLARITY IN YOUR RELATIONSHIPS WITH OTHERS IS TO ESTABLISH CLARITY WITH YOURSELF.

Establishing clarity doesn't happen overnight because we are always evolving, maturing, and growing as individuals. But there is something super sexy and attractive about someone who is comfortable in their own skin. And humans are excellent at picking up on confidence and authenticity. When you are clear on your value and who you are as a person, and you can show up authentically, your relationship will reflect that. Confident, authentic people can and will always have more quality choices in relationships.

Having self-confidence and established clarity doesn't mean you won't attract difficult or incompatible people or have relationship challenges. But when you are clear on who you are and what you are willing and unwilling to accept, it will help give you a starting point for navigating your relationship challenges. Then, as you continue dating, you will be able to see your way out of unhealthy relationships and see your way into healthy ones.

Love Check-In:
- What is/was your relationship like with your mom/dad, primary caregivers?
- How did they make you feel growing up? Was it healthy, secure, loving, unloving, difficult, etc.?
- What did you feel was missing with your caregivers that you may seek out or reinforce in your romantic relationships?
- What were some moments throughout your life where you were able to show up as yourself? How did that make you feel? And how did you feel during moments when you weren't being yourself?

LOVE MANTRA

Self-love governs the love you're willing to receive and accept from others.

2

THE NAKED TRUTH ABOUT SELF-LOVE: IT'S NOT JUST ABOUT LOVING YOURSELF

I want to share with you what I have learned and observed that creates healthy relationship dynamics with others and yourself. My thoughts on what works are based on my own personal experiences, my observations of happy and satisfying relationships that lasted multiple decades, and the success I have experienced with coaching people to cultivate healthier, happier, and more rewarding relationships.

Learn to love you. Learn to love you. Learn to love you.

This is so important! Make it your mantra. If you are not in love with yourself, then why in the world should someone else love you? It makes you much more attractive and appealing to others.

The power of self-love is real. I have witnessed this in myself and in other people in healthy relationships. Self-love is transformational, and both strange and wonderful things can happen when you learn to love and accept yourself. Self-love is not just repeating to yourself how much you love yourself, even though you may be pretty wonderful. Self-love is learning to love who you are *completely*, flaws and all. It's the ability to have humility, humor, and grace with yourself. It's about not making excuses when you recognize you have fallen into patterns that are detrimental to yourself and the relationships you enter into and encounter.

> BOTH STRANGE AND WONDERFUL THINGS CAN HAPPEN WHEN YOU LEARN TO LOVE AND ACCEPT YOURSELF.

Self-love is also about self-accountability. It's about breaking unhealthy patterns because of the respect you have for yourself. When you learn to flex the muscle of self-love, you move differently. You know you're not perfect, but you own it authentically. When you love yourself, you begin to recognize your beauty—not just in a superficial way but underneath the surface. You see your value. So you focus on yourself holistically, not just on your flaws, and you start to recognize the power of the battle scars that have, in fact, made you stronger and wiser and helped you to see things differently.

Think of fairy tales. We are often drawn to the character that is vulnerable and open with what they lack. We see their beauty on the inside and out before they fully recognize it. But we love it most when they find their strength! It's the balance of those two energies—recognizing your strengths, honoring and owning your vulnerabilities—that makes them even more appealing to us.

When you step into self-love and couple it with self-accountability, you can't help but attract new people into your life. It feels strange at first because the world—and your options—start to look completely different. While you may have first thought there weren't enough quality men or women available, self-love starts to elevate the type of men and women who are attracted to you. And if you're already in a relationship, self-love can be a magnet for your significant other because they recognize your value. Like energy attracts like energy, and all this new attention can feel strange—but completely liberating too!

WHEN YOU STEP INTO SELF-LOVE AND COUPLE IT WITH SELF-ACCOUNTABILITY, YOU CAN'T HELP BUT ATTRACT NEW PEOPLE INTO YOUR LIFE.

Maybe you have noticed how you are more drawn to people when you can tell they value themselves. Have you noticed how even (some of) their flaws seem attractive and endearing?

Accepting your flaws and those of others may seem counterintuitive; after all, much is derived from images that seem to project perfection. While we may be initially drawn to beauty and perfection in others, it is often when we see moments of imperfection and vulnerability that a person becomes more real and connective for us.

It's become a trend for people to share facets of themselves that are less than perfect. Brené Brown is extremely popular because she has done many talks about vulnerability—something with which we can all connect. However, the reason we connect with Brené on this topic is because she is often expressing her own vulnerable moments too.

When we see someone powerful and successful relay a story of vulnerability, it draws us closer to them. It makes them feel more relatable and more authentic. And when you see someone's authenticity, you automatically hone in on this, and it makes the person seem even more attractive. That's because being vulnerable requires courage. And courage is attractive!

BEING VULNERABLE REQUIRES COURAGE.

Each of us has flaws and faults. These are like elephants in the room. They stomp around unmentioned, and it makes everyone uncomfortable—unless you embrace them as part of who you are as a person. When you reveal and acknowledge who you are fully, you become more relatable. And when you are more relatable, you become more endearing, attractive, and interesting. Embrace those elephants!

When you are good with all aspects of yourself, people will bond to you, relate to you, and find you more real. Even if you reveal things that may not be so appealing, others will feel compassion for you. Showing some vulnerability inherently makes us more likeable, relatable, and real to others. This is because every one of us struggles with some kind of self-perceived insecurity, flaw, or weakness, and we all want validation that we are okay despite our imperfections.

Learning to be with yourself and have fun by yourself is *powerful*. When you fully understand who you are and what you bring to the table—including all the good, the bad, and the ugly—this will make you much more attractive to others. Self-confidence, self-love, and self-accountability give you more appeal than faux perfection. Combined, these "self" characteristics help you dial into what is valuable about yourself and allow you to break patterns that could be keeping you from the relationship you want and deserve.

Look ... even superheroes have flaws. Superman wants to fit in and appear normal to Lois Lane. Batman longs to save the family he feels guilty for losing at such a young age, and he laments what he could have done to change the outcome. The Incredible Hulk wants to control himself; he just wants to be Bruce—a normal guy. We notice flaws in our favorite superheroes, but it doesn't turn us away. We still admire them. In fact, we respect their bravery even more because we know they are vulnerable.

Like us.

A close friend of mine was sharing his perspective on dating, and I was struck by his candid observation. He was speaking about what kind of woman he and other guys find most attractive. He stated that women are sometimes surprised by men's choices in mates because guys are often drawn to and date women who may not be viewed as conventionally attractive by society's standards. These men are drawn to women who feel comfortable with themselves and are happy in their own skin. Men, just like women, desire a deeper connection and are attracted to those who are multidimensional and multifaceted. It's not all about physical attractiveness!

Confidence is attractive because it shows that you are in tune with yourself, you know what you will or will not accept, and you live life on your own terms. This means having a romantic partner in your life is not something you look at as a necessity. In your mind, you are okay in your own right,

> **YOUR SIGNIFICANT OTHER IS THE CHERRY ON TOP—NOT THE ICE CREAM.**

regardless of whether you have a significant other or not. Your significant other is the cherry on top—not the ice cream.

When we are happy, we draw positive people and energy to us naturally; it is effortless. However, when we have too much negative energy or are unsure or insecure, the opposite happens. We draw negative energy into our circle, and people appear who carry this same type of energy. Think about it. Oftentimes when we have a bad morning and think or state that it's going to be a bad day, our words become a self-fulfilling prophecy. For example, you may start off the morning with your alarm not going off as expected, setting you behind for the day. It might disrupt your schedule, your kids' schedule, your work schedule, etc., setting you up to feel that everything will just get worse from then on. On these types of days when something goes wrong, it's easy to fall into a gloom-and-doom mood and start focusing on everything that goes wrong.

When we're having a bad day, it can be easy to forget that there are many good things going on too. I'm not telling you to fall into a habit of toxic positivity, because I do believe it's very normal to have days that feel rougher than others. However, it's more beneficial to have your moment and then move forward. Lamenting and ruminating sets you up for a vicious cycle of negativity. And the reality is, most us don't want to be around someone who is negative the majority of the time.

The same applies to who we attract and the energy we attract. Our state of mind and being is transferable; people pick up on it. When you aren't feeling your best, you often draw people with a similar energy. On the other hand, when you feel like you're on top of the world, it's interesting to look at the type of people who are drawn to you. In moments like that, it's almost like you can't get enough interaction from others, because that energy feels good and everybody wants more of it. In fact, that friend of yours with the negative energy might even want to engage with you because, ironically, even *they* don't want to be around people with negative or toxic energy. So they may want to borrow some of your positive energy—but don't let them! In other words, don't allow someone with toxic energy to spoil your day.

With that in mind, think back over your dating history. Think about the best relationships you've ever had. What was your frame of mind during those time periods? Who were you attracting? What were their traits?

Now think back to a negative relationship and what your frame of mind was like during that period of time. What types of people did you attract? What were they like?

Like most people, I have experienced both sides of the coin. When my frame of mind was not in the right place, I attracted partners who were not good for me. For example, I would often attract men who were emotionally unavailable. But after some soul searching and developing more self-awareness, I realized I wasn't making *myself* fully available either. I was drawn to these men because they made me comfortable with not being vulnerable. It was like a self-fulfilling prophecy; I wasn't available, so I subconsciously sought out people who were in the same headspace. They kept me in a place where I didn't have to address or deal with my vulnerability in a relationship. It felt safer, but in reality it was limiting my ability to truly connect in a meaningful, long-lasting relationship—which is what I really wanted. I kept choosing these guys because I wasn't ready to bare myself fully after having been so hurt in past relationships where I was truly open. I thought I was protecting myself, but I was actually *preventing* myself from being in a fulfilling relationship. I was getting in my own way. If I had never learned to lean into my vulnerability, I would have been stuck repeating the same pattern over and over again.

I refer to this period as my "dating dark ages."

The next time you are at a party, take notice of which woman or man receives the most attention. Maybe it will surprise you. Because it may not be the best-looking woman or the guy with the perfect body. Rather, it could be an average-looking person, but one who is able to be him- or herself. They present an energy that makes others want to be around them. This energy comes from the confidence of knowing who they are, what they bring to the table, their value. And this positive energy creates an irresistible force field. Their magnetism draws an array of suitors to them. Hello, Clark Kent!

POSITIVE ENERGY CREATES AN IRRESISTIBLE FORCE FIELD.

Let's talk about what it looks like when someone doesn't present as confident. They are given a compliment, but they shut it down or make an excuse for the compliment. They are asked their opinion or preference about something but constantly defer to others as opposed to expressing their views. Their body language makes them seem as though they aren't sure if they fit or even belong in the room. They seek reassurance from others to the point you can't tell what they feel, think, or believe—there is no individuality! Are you starting to get the gist? Please don't do this!

Now let's talk about what confidence looks like and its effect on others. It's easy to observe this for yourself. Next time you are at a work function, bar, club, or party, be observant. Do a little investigative work. Notice who catches your eye, the person you think will shake up the room, anyone there who seems to exude attractive energy. They may have an awkwardness to them that is appealing and makes them attractive. For example, some people like people who are a bit nerdy and bookish, and when that nerd lets that shine, they may be surprised by who they attract. A person may have a great sense of humor. Or they could be a little corny. Some people like people with offbeat humor. Or it could be the way they have an infectious laugh or interact in their conversations with others. Maybe it's the way they take care of everyone in the room. Perhaps they are highly aware of others around them, and they are that person who checks in on how people are doing and feeling, and they keep the energy positive in the room, etc.

Now watch what happens to that individual. Pay attention to who interacts with them, the people who surround them, and how much attention they receive. No matter their unique characteristics, what makes this person attractive is how they show up as their authentic self. And the qualities they exhibit make them endearing to others, adding to their level of attractiveness.

IT'S NOT WHAT YOU LOOK LIKE BUT HOW YOU LIKE YOURSELF.

See? It's not what you look like but how you like yourself.

So be comfortable with the skin you are in. Embrace and be confident about your flaws. You are enough; you have value on your own. A relationship will not complete you. A good and healthy relationship will only serve to complement who you already are.

SELF-LOVE MANTRA

I love myself completely for who I am and how I am. I may be different from others, but that is okay because I am okay with me.

Love Check-In
The Confidence Test

For Single Folks:
Find two people—one who exudes attractive energy and one who doesn't.
- What did you observe about each of them?
- What was attractive?
- What was unattractive?
- How might you apply these observations and characteristics to your own life?

For Couples:
- What drew you to your significant other?
- What do you find attractive?
- What keeps you engaged in your relationship?

3

FORGET THE FAIRY TALE: THE REALITY OF WHAT A HEALTHY RELATIONSHIP LOOKS LIKE

> **HEALTHY RELATIONSHIP MANTRA**
> "We must be willing to learn our spouse's primary love language if we are to be effective communicators of love."
> —GARY CHAPMAN, *The 5 Love Languages: The Secret to Love that Lasts*

Stay Away from Interpretation Mode

Sometimes relationships are hard because we *make* them hard. Too often we make assumptions about our partners rather than ask them directly about their intentions. When our significant other exhibits a certain behavior, fails to take a specific action toward us, or acts a certain way, we may go into *interpretation mode*.

What does this mean? It means you interpret the other person's actions based on how you would feel or act instead of asking why the person exhibited the specific action.

For example, in the early phases of my relationship with my now husband, when he would give me gifts, his expectation was that I would react a certain way. He wanted to know how excited I was about the gift and how well he had done in choosing it. Gifting was his way of showing how much he loved and cared about me. In this regard, I failed *epically* at first. You see, my excitement was more of a thank you and a hug and a kiss; I didn't exactly jump around with glee. But upon observing his family members and how they responded when someone gave *them* a gift, it gave me tremendous insight into why my husband looked for a certain reaction. When gifts are exchanged in his family, people become incredibly excited. They express a heartfelt and hearty reaction. They will jump around, yell out their appreciation and thanks, hug wholeheartedly—it's a love fest! You feel like you bought them the best gift ever. It's adorable!

Experiencing my new family's reactions helped me to understand why my more muted reaction was giving my husband weird vibes after he had so thoughtfully picked out a gift for me. Once I discovered this, I shared my observation with him so he would understand. But more importantly, I made sure that from then on, I demonstrated to him my appreciativeness of the gift—in the way he expected. This small adjustment on my part helped my husband to see I was pleased with his gifts, and I learned that gifting was one of his love languages.[1] Can you imagine how this could have played out if I hadn't taken time to learn and understand his expectations?

---

[1] Gary Chapman's book *The 5 Love Languages: The Secret to Love that Lasts* is a great read whether you're just starting out or are in a committed relationship. Chapman's approach can help you to determine what drives you in a relationship.

The same is true of any relationship in which expectations are unclear. If your partner doesn't respond to your words or actions in a way you expect, you may automatically assume their intentions are negative and thoughtless. You may feel hurt, rejected, or unloved. But is this really the case? Or are your feelings centered on your own interpretations and expectations? Why not ask your partner why they chose to respond in this way? They may have a good reason. Maybe they were actually trying to please you, or this is what they did growing up in their family, or they believed it was what you wanted.

We all tend to see things through our own prisms. This is how we live, experience, and understand things. However, you can learn a lot when you step outside of your own interpretations. Doing so can start you down a different road. You may begin to have more realistic expectations in a relationship.

This is the path to relationship success.

Bitter Versus Sweet

Now bear with me a second here and think of your parents—or other close friends or family—and their relationship with you. They may know you better than anyone else does. Yet you probably have times in which you feel like they do not know you at all. This feeling resonates during the teenage years and may remain in adulthood.

Compare this with someone who you're in a relationship with (current, past, or future). They have known you for a short period of time compared to your parents, and yet you have expectations that this person will be able to figure you out. You give them hints, limited interactions, and nonverbal cues, and you still expect them to know what you want from them at all times.

Kinda unfair, don't you think?

It's *so* important to set realistic expectations in a relationship. Early on, you should discuss with your partner where you want to head in your relationship, your values, whether you want to be monogamous, and other issues that are essential to you personally.

> IT'S *SO* IMPORTANT TO SET REALISTIC EXPECTATIONS IN A RELATIONSHIP.

And later, if things become more serious, you can ask them about their vision of what marriage or a committed relationship should be and how they want to raise kids if the two of you have them. Everyone has a fantasy in their mind of what a perfect relationship looks like, and if you can delve into this sooner rather than later, it will do a lot toward helping you to create realistic expectations and goals. These are factors that will either place you on the same journey or make you run on opposite paths.

You should not expect your partner to understand your feelings automatically, especially in the beginning. He or she will not know exactly what to do each and every time to make you happy. If you're disappointed when they don't live up to your unrealistic expectations, this will set you up for a bitter relationship. And even as time progresses, it's important to lean into curiosity and ask your partner about their expectations. We all evolve, and what someone may have valued earlier can change over time with new experiences or significant changes in their life.

Many people I observed and have coached who want to be more intentional in their relationships have found that writing out a visual list of the nonnegotiable qualities they want in their significant others is helpful. I use this technique often with clients I coach. It provides a visual frame of reference and helps them to hone in more specifically on what they want in a relationship. Sometimes until you have that clarity, it can make it difficult for you to understand what you value most in a relationship. But when you have this down in a visual reference, it becomes a powerful tool to provide gentle guidance and intentionality in what you pursue in your relationships.

I did this for myself when I wanted to have more clarity as to the type of person I felt would be most compatible for me. I called it my Love List. My Love List enabled me to recognize the traits and expectations I desired for my next relationship. Before I met my now husband, I wrote down a list of qualities and attributes of what I desired in a mate. I included tangible ones: spiritual, stable, consistent, good work ethic, etc. And I included intangible ones: humility, compassion, humor, etc.

I also had in my list the things that I really didn't desire (and no judgement to you if you match any of these attributes): smoker, unstable, unwilling to engage in therapy if needed, etc. For me, this became my bible as to how I viewed potential suitors. It helped me to eliminate people who weren't on the same page sooner because I was being more intentional about who I wanted to be and who I wanted in my life.

I still made some missteps along the way. And often those missteps were when I completely deviated from the tangible and intangible qualities I was seeking. However, when I walked away from those relationships or they didn't work out, I had more self-awareness that these relationships weren't the ones for me. My Love List helped provide me with steady guidance and kept me from straying toward relationships that wouldn't give me what I had already determined I needed and desired.

The key was keeping the attributes realistic and focusing on intangible qualities that would matter when the chips were down in our relationship, when things were difficult. This focus provided clarity, direction, and a realistic approach to finding the right person for me.

And for me, dating, and later my relationship with my husband, became easier. I am able to use my original list, even now, to reflect back on why my husband and I started down this road and keep those qualities at the top of my mind when we're navigating tough moments. I was pleasantly surprised to learn after marrying my husband that he had his own Love List of what he was looking for in a partner too! It further solidified to me that we were both being very intentional about the type of relationship and person we wanted in our lives. And we were creating a foundation by first establishing to ourselves what we were prioritizing in a relationship so we would recognize those kinds of people when they showed up in our lives.

You might want to make a Love List for yourself. It will keep you honest, focused, and intentional in your relationship journey—and even once you are in a relationship! Your Love List can be flexible, but understanding what is important to you will help you to stay away from potential partners who do not meet the standards you require for a relationship.

For example, say you have a strong spiritual belief that affects your lifestyle choices, and it's important that the other person have similar beliefs and views. You may want to incorporate this belief system into how you raise your kids or how you live your life day to day. With your list in mind, you can avoid getting involved with somebody who doesn't share the same beliefs. Instead of attempting to change the other person's mind, you can turn your focus to someone else—a potential partner who is more aligned to your own goals. This can only occur if you establish ahead of time that your spirituality is one of your nonnegotiables.

We all have heard the horror stories. We all know people who have sacrificed their nonnegotiables and ended up with someone who is not a good fit. We all know sad people who feel cheated and not fulfilled in their relationship.

They are not on the path to a healthy relationship. In order to break the pattern of connecting to relationships that are unhealthy, it's important for us to understand who we are first. This piece is at the core of our foundation for a healthy relationship. If we are unsure of what our value is, what values are important to us, and the role we see a relationship playing in our life, it becomes easier for us to remain in relationships that do not serve us.

So make your Love List and check it twice. And don't look for someone who meets your expectations until your list is done. That way, you can hit the ground running and have greater clarity when you meet the person with whom you want to spend your life.

RELATIONSHIP REALISM MANTRA
I will set and maintain realistic expectations in my relationship.

Love Check-In
Relationship Expectations

For Single Folks:
- What patterns have worked well in your previous relationships?
- Which traits and expectations are must-haves?
- What core values are important to you in your relationship?

For Couples:
- How are we meeting our expectations we established for our relationships? What are we doing well?
- How have our expectations changed and how can we adjust to meet them?
- What are some expectations we want to add to make our relationship more fulfilling for both of us?

4

NO ONE IS PERFECT, EVEN YOU: BUILDING A HEALTHY AND REWARDING RELATIONSHIP

*D*id you make the list of nonnegotiables? If so, you are well aware of the traits you want in a partner. But take another look at your list. If you have listed *too* many qualifications, you might be overlooking potential partners who could make you happy.

Is it time to redo your list?

In the age of high-tech dating, with access to a multitude of dating websites, apps, and social media, it seems easier than ever before to be choosy about partners. With so many potential partners readily available, you may find that you are even more picky than before when choosing someone to date. But this kind of selectivity can be overdone and may eliminate the *best* relationships from your list of options.

Perfect Versus Perfect for You

The key is to be realistic. You may need to let go of some of your requirements. Does he have to drive a specific car or work in a specific profession? Is that particular salary range a must? Do you really need a mate with Barbie doll measurements? Are height and weight really nonnegotiable? Such picky standards can limit your options. Remember: narrow criteria, narrower choices. Don't box yourself in!

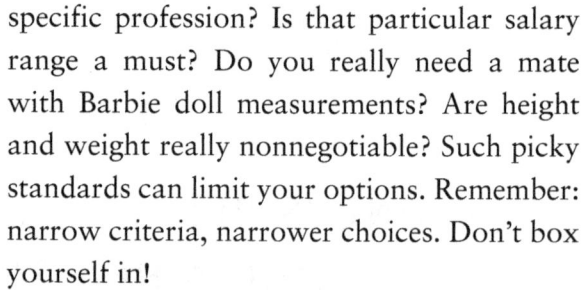

REMEMBER: NARROW CRITERIA, NARROWER CHOICES. DON'T BOX YOURSELF IN!

It's important to have standards, to know what you need. But this should be tempered with a dose of realism. After all, *you are not perfect.* No one is! We all have our imperfections, our areas of weakness. Each of us has our appealing and not-so-appealing traits. Why should we expect to find a partner who is perfect if we aren't perfect ourselves?

We all need to give ourselves the time and space to accept our weaknesses, then work on strengthening them so we can grow and evolve. And we need to remember this when looking for our significant others. Pay attention to the little things, but don't overanalyze them. Don't be too quick to reject someone. Take your time and give each person ample consideration.

Now say you meet someone and he is nice, easy to talk to, and is enjoying a successful career … but he does not have all the physical attributes you regard as your ideal type. If he vibes with you in the other areas, are you going to sacrifice the connection because he isn't as tall or handsome as you might have wanted? Because if you already dated other men who *were* tall and handsome and you failed to connect with them on an emotional level or had little in common with them, can it really hurt to try something different?

In matters of the heart, we often have a tendency to focus on the external first, then the internal. However, it's important to see a person for who they are wholly; you have to learn to truly read a person, not just judge the book by its cover. Because in the long term, who the person is, how you interact with them, and how they complement you will be what brings totality to the relationship—along with the external traits like height, weight, salary, and looks. But it's their internal characteristics that will drive the relationship for the long run.

Don't get me wrong; external traits are important too. Most of the initial attraction between two people is physical in nature, and that is normal. But the external component will fade eventually and can be altered suddenly due to health, accidents, aging, and other factors. And looking at the other side of the coin, what if *you* were the person who was valued only on an external level? Would you want to be with someone who was just into your looks or income rather than your most valuable assets?

Think of it from this perspective: External plays some significance but is short term. Internal is long term and indicative of how a couple will evolve in a relationship. We all want to be loved for who we really are, right? Our internal factors are what determine who we will be in the long term.

Looking at someone holistically is important because we are with the whole person, not just certain aspects of them. Often I have heard men and women be surprised by someone who seemingly has it together but lacks emotional maturity. This person may be highly successful but can't navigate having a serious conversation or being able to go deeper and show up for the other person emotionally, which can stunt the relationship.

While financial stability is important, it's important to make sure that people are developed emotionally, mentally, sexually, and spiritually too! Each facet will play into your relationship and its ability to survive the downturns and mature over time. As you seek out a potential mate, evaluate all of these facets. You will need every piece to navigate your relationship with them. And if you are already in a relationship, note that while you and your significant other may be strong in certain areas, there are opportunities for continued development to strengthen your relationship. Sometimes one person may be stronger than the other in an area and can help bring the other person along. No one is perfect, but I do believe you can look to these facets of a person to gauge where you need to build, learn, and grow together.

The "It Factor"

There are other factors that play into your attraction to someone. One of these is the "it factor." You know, that special trait someone has that draws you closer, the one you just can't explain. But when you feel it, it just feels *right*. For example, when you have dated people with whom you naturally connected, you may have noticed a few things that happened during the process. Maybe it was easier to communicate with them, or you felt you could show aspects of yourself you would normally try to hide. Or perhaps you noticed a natural flow and connection that didn't feel forced. Of course there may still be moments of difficulty even in this kind of relationship, but there is also a special space in which you feel comfortable, unguarded, and in tune.

The "it factor" magnifies other feelings you have for a person. When somebody is "it," they feel like somebody you can be around for the longer term, and that feeling can, for some, be immediate. But sometimes it can take time to cultivate that feeling. In the early phases of dating, and even early in a marriage, you are in the infancy or discovery phase of your relationship. This is also called the "honeymoon" phase of the relationship because everything feels perfect. It's easy to get caught up in the feel-good feelings at the beginning of a relationship, and that can often overshadow things we may not pay close attention to initially. For example, when things are going well in the early phases of a relationship, we may not pay close attention to someone who has a bad temper. We may rule it out as them having a moment, even though the way they react to someone or an instance is unacceptable. This bad temper may not be apparent or problematic until it resurfaces directed toward us or consistently we see this person cannot manage their temper. It's easy to ignore these telltale signs during the honeymoon phase because during that phase we're less guarded or maybe think the behavior is a one-off situation.

It's hard to see things clearly in the early phases of a relationship because that is often when chemistry is more intense. It's also why it's important to recognize that chemistry in the early phases of a relationship isn't always a predictor of relationship success. Chemistry can send us some false signals and can sometimes even be a red flag in a relationship.

> **CHEMISTRY CAN SEND US SOME FALSE SIGNALS AND CAN SOMETIMES EVEN BE A RED FLAG IN A RELATIONSHIP.**

Copy that?

Slow and Steady

Many solid relationships exist in which couples did not click at first but over time proved to be successful. We've all dated people who we felt lacked qualities we thought we needed for the long term. Maybe we initially thought they were not tall or thin enough, they were kinda boring, or that nothing jumped out and made us go "Wow." But then maybe we gave them additional chances and found them to be more likeable as time progressed.

The chemistry of immediate attraction does not always occur with the best relationship partners. It happens more naturally with some people, and it doesn't always happen as quickly as you would like it to. Think of the tortoise and the hare: both get to their destinations, but their *approach* is different. In relationships, a steady and consistent pace of growing and getting to know each other can be better and more sustainable than a quick start. That slower development gives you time to get to know the other person, to understand them on a deeper level, and to assess as to whether they are the right fit for you.

It is too easy to eliminate someone quickly when you first start dating. Instead, take time to see what develops. And if you are already in a relationship, one that needs work, why not continue to give it a chance? Try to remember why you were initially attracted, then go from there. In relationships, there's always room for growth and improvement.

I know it's tempting to jump or move on to the next person, but I feel when you do this, you are shortcutting yourself from building healthy relationship habits. There is a discovery phase in a relationship where you need time to get to know the other person. By putting in quality time, it allows you to get there with them.

Discovery is an important part of relationship building, another one of those factors that create your strong relationship foundation.

Building and solidifying a relationship takes time. When you forsake putting time into a relationship, you shortcut the process. Don't be a hare! If something feels right—whether you feel the initial "it factor" or you get there slowly and steadily—take your time, assess, continue to feel, and see how things develop. Doing so, even if *that* relationship doesn't work out, will help you in the long term to have healthier, more satisfying relationships.

> DISCOVERY IS AN IMPORTANT PART OF RELATIONSHIP BUILDING.

Remember, relationships are built; they're not a given.

We all can appreciate the person who's there for us when we're in the beginning stages of building something. We all value a partner who can be supportive, love us for who we are, help us to evolve, and provide constructive feedback. We all need someone who can be both a friend *and* a lover. And this can lead to a relationship that is perfect. Not *perfect* perfect, but perfect for our own individual needs.

So be open. Know what you want, but understand you might meet a diamond in the rough—and that's okay! After the relationship takes off, you might just be rewarded for your patience and support during the process. Slow and steady wins the relationship race!

Love Check-In
Relationship Expectations Take Two: The Less Picky Version!

For Singles:
- Get out your pen and paper or use your tablet to jot down a list of five to ten desirable attributes you want in a partner.
- What can you live with, and what can you absolutely not deal with related to your partner?
- When have these attributes worked well in your relationships? When haven't they and why?

For Couples:
- What are the attributes you like about your partner?
- What attributes initially drew you to your partner?
- What attributes make you want to remain in this relationship?
- What are the traits you two are struggling with in each other, and is there a way to compromise on any of these?

ACCEPTANCE MANTRA
I will be picky, just not too daggone picky, when choosing my mate!

5

THE HEALTHY RELATIONSHIP ROAD MAP: HOW TO NAVIGATE YOUR RELATIONSHIP ROADBLOCKS

> **HEALTHY RELATIONSHIP MANTRA**
>
> I will not compare my relationship to others'. Our relationship dynamic just needs to work for the two of us.

Explore Your Path to a Healthy Relationship: Let Positive Role Models Guide the Way

The great thing about relationships is you can create your own story. However, it can't hurt to borrow some tips and tricks from others whose relationships are thriving. If you come from a family background with divorce or trauma, then obviously you do not want to model the relationship behavior you observed growing up. You want a partnership that is healthier and longer lasting. Fortunately, you can learn from other relationships as well. You can be a relationship detective, exploring and studying those who are doing it right.

Start by identifying some of the healthy relationships you've observed in your life. Think about the couples you know who have a tight bond and mutual understanding. There are probably some couples you want to model and others you don't. Are you friends with a couple who seem to know how to bring out the best in each other? Have you noticed that they don't compete with each other but do a good job of supporting and building each other up? Ask them how they reached this point. Or if you notice a couple who navigates through touchy topics without alienating each other, but they are still able to express their viewpoints, observe how they do so or inquire as to what they have found to be effective for disagreeing with their partner in a respectful way.

Look at those model couples. Ask them how they handle disagreements. Observe how they manage parenting their kids. Inquire as to how they have learned to communicate effectively. Notice if they are respectful to each other and how they demonstrate it. Do they display affection—and how? Are they complimentary to each other? How do their differences help make their relationship better?

Speaking of differences, it's important to recognize that in a partnership, two people come together with different skill sets. This is a good thing! One person may be an amazing planner with the ability to schedule things out months in advance, while the other may make decisions in the moment. However, when both skill sets come together, while it might feel uncomfortable on both sides, if both partners learn to lean into each other's strengths, this collaboration can create a mix of some structure and spontaneity. The bottom line is that in a relationship, iron sharpens iron. When a couple learns to use their strengths together, they, in turn, can see problems, challenges, and issues that emerge from different angles. So observe others in healthy relationships, even in those couples who you see as role models. How do their strengths/differences complement one another? How do they work together to use their respective strengths? How do these differences come in handy during conflicts? Or how do differences sometimes contribute toward conflicts?

No couple is *on* 24/7. No matter what anyone says, there is always going to be some level of conflict in every relationship. And some conflicts might go unresolved, but successful couples can live with this. Even a couple in a long-term, long-lasting, healthy relationship may not agree on everything. In fact, this is pretty common! My parents, who were married for fifty-seven years, often said there were things they had to agree to disagree on. They both realized that as long as these topics weren't harmful to their overall relationship, it was perfectly acceptable for them to see things differently. Now if these differences are things that impact the quality of the relationship—e.g., raising kids a particular way, religious differences, core values relating to the relationship—a couple needs to re-evaluate the relationship and determine if they can find a way to compromise or meet in the middle. If they can't, they may have to make different decisions pertaining to the relationship.

There are telltale signs for when a couple is happily cohabitating and when this is not the case. Pay attention to body language and other nonverbal cues. Do you see couples laughing together and speaking more so about each other's positive attributes? Do you see them offering constructive criticism to each other in a way that helps to build up the other person and in a respectful way? Or do you see a couple constantly demeaning each other or looking for opportunities to tear down each other? These seemingly small things are often larger indicators of the difference in couples who focus in on each other's positive attributes, which allows them to have a more satisfying relationship, versus couples who constantly tear down each other. There is a balance. It's not that the couple highlighting each other's positive attributes more so doesn't see or recognize their significant other's deficits. It's more so that they are building on each other's strengths and continuing to work through the murky aspects too. Another strong indicator of a healthy relationship is each person being who they truly are without altering their personality. But if you have to change who you are and you can't show up as your authentic self, it's incredibly difficult to have a fulfilling partnership.

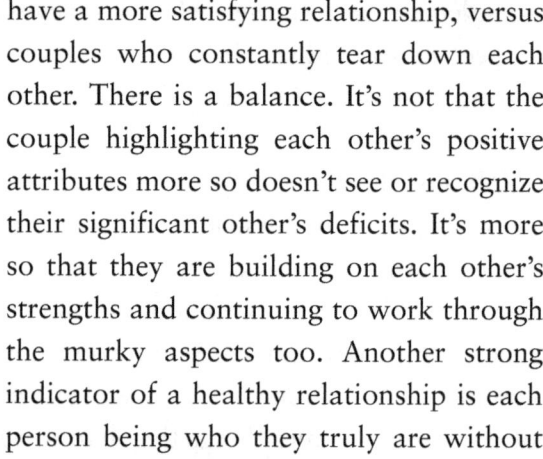

IF YOU HAVE TO CHANGE WHO YOU ARE AND YOU CAN'T SHOW UP AS YOUR AUTHENTIC SELF, IT'S INCREDIBLY DIFFICULT TO HAVE A FULFILLING PARTNERSHIP.

Many years ago I attended a holiday party for work, and we had been told to bring our significant others. I could tell who was comfortable with their spouse; these individuals behaved the same way they did when they were at work with their colleagues. For example, one guy I worked with was a huge flirt in the office. He was harmless but flirty—a big jokester. When I interacted with him and his wife at the party, he continued to display his flirtatious behaviors. His behavior was a bit surprising to me. Disrespectful? In this case, no, because she laughed too. That flirtatiousness was part of who he was, and his wife had accepted that about him. In fact, this might have been what drew her to him, the "it factor" for her. She told me she knew his heart was in the right place with her.

I realized this was a dynamic in their relationship that worked *for them*, but each couple is their own entity. Each couple has their own way of interacting, understanding, and relating to each other.

At this same party, I observed other people who looked uncomfortable with their significant others. I could tell who wasn't attuned to their partner, who seemed tense, and who wasn't comfortable with interacting or communicating with each other in this social scenario. I noticed one co-worker who was a completely different person when his wife was present. He seemed uneasy showing up the way he normally did at work. He was quiet, less playful, and less engaged. He stuck close by his wife the entire time and looked oddly distressed. It was a stark contrast to others whose personalities seemed consistent with or without their significant others, and it was clear that he didn't feel comfortable.

While it may be immediately apparent to others when a couple doesn't seem comfortable with each other, surprisingly, it may not always be as obvious to the couple themselves. Sometimes this inability to act like ourselves can be a blind spot.

You may be wondering, how can I create self-awareness around my relationship blind spots? Here are a few ideas. I often coach my clients to do a Relationship Inventory. Look back at your past (or current) relationships and assess what you felt was a common theme. Did you feel like yourself when you were with your partner? Do you feel stuck in similar relationship patterns? Or do you seem to attract the wrong people for you? If you have some exes with whom you are friends, ask them directly what they thought were your positive attributes and the things they thought may have hampered your relationship. And while it may be tempting to ask your friends or family members what they think are some of your strengths and weaknesses in past relationships, people who are in the actual relationship with us see us in a different light than our friends or family do. And often their experience and insight come from a different perspective and are based on their experiences with relationships. It's not that their intentions aren't in the right place, but someone in a relationship with you is interacting with you in a totally different way.

I know this suggestion may feel odd, but what I think you will uncover are common threads that will give you more self-awareness around your relationship blind spots. Exes have nothing to lose, so while this exercise might seem painful, it will give you incredible insights. Jot it down in your journal or on paper, voice memo it, or use your tablet to make note of your findings. There is incredible power in actually writing something down that helps it to register into our conscious and subconscious behavior. Doing this exercise will not only provide insight into how you can improve your relationship blind spots but also see those qualities in others as you enter into new or strengthen your current relationships.

It can take time, effort, and experience to learn what a healthy relationship looks like versus a toxic one, but you don't have to figure this out by yourself. You can do something similar to help you learn how to cultivate healthier relationships. Find a couple you have observed who exhibit a healthy relationship in communicating, supporting, and showing up for one another. Just like when you start a job and you want to do your best and be at the top of your game, it helps to seek out someone who is successful to mentor you. Watch them, then use what you think may work for you and your potential—or current—significant other. However, be sure to exercise some caution here. As I've mentioned before, no couple has a perfect relationship, and that is important to realize as you observe others in action. Pay close attention to the more important things, such as the way the other person handles their ups and downs and how they navigate difficult situations and circumstances. This can give you some solid ideas on how you and your significant other can handle both the good and the bad times in your own relationship. Observe and then customize what may work for you and your significant other. And be careful not to judge someone else's relationship. Instead, try to understand how each relationship is unique to the parties involved. Ask questions. How do you do it? How do you make your relationship work? Your investigations will pay off for your future relationship success.

There is little rhyme or reason to relationships, and there is no one size fits all that works for everyone. Each relationship has its own rhythm. It can be a mystery as to why some relationships click and others don't. However, I assure you: relationships that are more rewarding and healthy have some things in common.

We all may struggle in some ways to keep our relationships going. But if we are more honest about this, we might be able to help each other through these normal relationship struggles.

Love Check-In

For Singles:
- Write down five ways you would like to build a partnership with your partner.
- What are three things in relationships where you were on the same page with your partner that you wouldn't have accomplished on your own?

For Couples:
- If your relationship is hitting tough spots and you can't get past them, try counseling or find someone you trust who is in a long-term relationship. Ask them what is working for them and how they navigate difficult moments.
- Find a couples retreat and try it out. Seek out a retreat that incorporates couples similar to you and your significant other. It can help to broaden your relationships with other couples who may be experiencing similar challenges.

> **HEALTHY RELATIONSHIP MANTRA**
>
> I will model healthy relationships and customize what works best for my partner and me. No relationship is perfect. My goal is to learn from others in order to strengthen my own relationship.

6

THE POWER OF TEAMWORK: THE COMMON FACTOR FOR A HAPPY AND HEALTHY RELATIONSHIP

> **HEALTHY RELATIONSHIP MANTRA**
> Being in a relationship is like being on a team. Your team is only as strong as everyone on it.

Once you have applied the rules of building a healthy relationship—loving yourself, setting realistic expectations, remembering that people aren't perfect, and identifying roadblocks—you are well along the path of success. You are exhibiting healthy energy and, perhaps, attracting people with positive vibes. You know what you want and what your nonnegotiables are in the partner you will choose, leading to more viable choices. If you are already in a relationship, maybe you are now ready to move ahead by giving your relationship time and space to evolve. Whether your past relationships have encountered rough patches or you have experienced moments of feeling lost, you have identified these roadblocks and now have the skills to navigate past them. After everything is said and done, we desire happy and rewarding relationships. If you aspire to have this type of relationship, these are the common traits that healthy relationships share.

Operating as a Team Leads to a Relationship Dream
Everyone loves a relationship that's on fire. This kind of passion is fun and can keep things liberating, carefree, and easy. The challenge for most of us is when this same relationship evolves. As the relationship evolves, we might be less lenient because our expectations have shifted; as our significant others learn more about us, we expect more from them, and vice versa. So as we go through different challenges with them, the relationship changes, and there can even be moments where we have doubts.

For example, you might hit what I call the Everything Is a Fight era of your relationship. You just can't seem to agree on anything no matter how hard you try. You're frustrated and so is your significant other. You might even wonder if you made a mistake or may start to second guess that this is the relationship for you. But the reality is that every relationship will face some type of challenge. There will be difficult moments like these. They are normal, because the two of you are constantly changing, growing, and having different experiences that impact how you show up in the relationship. If couples can learn to navigate through these difficult moments, however, it can help them to build a stronger bond and a healthy foundation that can sustain them for the long term.

When you are clashing with your significant other, going through a particularly difficult time, or disagreeing about things, it can be tough to stay the course. During these times, it can be so tempting to leave the relationship. But before you leave, consider whether the situation is actually toxic or you've simply hit a speed bump. Here are some clues of when you may be hitting a speed bump versus being in an toxic or unhealthy relationship.

Perhaps you two are having disagreements about how you do things in the house—how it's cleaned or organized, who has what duties in the household—and you keep hitting an impasse. You may argue, but your language isn't disrespectful and no harm is done physically to the other person. These are norms in relationships because you are learning how to live with and accept each other and compromise on things. Your arguments might get heated, but there is room to compromise, and you will learn to do so.

On the other hand, if your partner is blatantly disrespectful of you, even when you tell them their behavior is hurtful, then your relationship is likely toxic. Maybe they're verbally or physically abusive. In these scenarios, you may need to seek out counseling to navigate whether the person can change their behavior or if their issues are unsolvable. If you are experiencing toxic situations or witnessing unhealthy behaviors, seek out the support of others to help you to get through it or, if necessary, remove yourself from the relationship.

Think of it this way: you and your significant other are a team. Teams stay together through it all. When it's good, teammates celebrate. When it's bad, they may cuss, shout, cry, and then support and comfort each other through the pain. When things are just okay, well, they're okay! But as any team knows, in order to win, you're going to have to go through some losses. These low times can be looked at as learning periods. Such times can help prepare you to handle and navigate the wins.

Unfortunately, good times can't exist without the bad, and in every relationship there will be a mix of great times and those that don't feel so great. No relationship is static. Your relationship will not stay the same—and this is a good thing! If a relationship never changes, no matter how great it is, one or both of you will grow bored with it.

Be a Team Player

Every teammate is different, and sometimes one person is not as attuned to the others, or maybe somebody is having a rough day. But when one team member is down, it affects everyone else. Disagreements may erupt more easily, and the team may even lose the match. This is all part of team play.

It's also part of being in a relationship.

As you begin a new relationship, remember what it means to be a TEAM: Together Everyone Achieves More. Think of a football team: when they are trying to get the ball to the red zone and score a touchdown, there's a series of things that needs to happen first. The quarterback has to find a wide receiver or running back to throw the ball. The quarterback needs protection from his offensive line so he can throw the ball to a wide receiver or running back and get the ball to the red zone. Each team member has a role to play in order to block other players from intercepting the ball and interrupting the wide receiver or running back from scoring a touchdown.

> **AS YOU BEGIN A NEW RELATIONSHIP, REMEMBER WHAT IT MEANS TO BE A TEAM: TOGETHER EVERYONE ACHIEVES MORE.**

Similarly, each person in a romantic relationship has to have the other's back as they navigate through different life scenarios together. For example, one partner may lose a parent, which can create tremendous grief and depression. It might be hard for the other person in the relationship to know how to show up for their partner who has just experienced a loss since grief is something people must resolve within themselves. These powerful emotions might put pressure on the relationship because the person who has experienced loss may seem less present, less attuned to their significant other, and may have some significant moments of emotional ups and downs. As another example, one partner may have challenges they face following addiction issues or past traumas. There may be periods when these past (or continuing) issues rise to the surface, altering the fabric of a happy relationship. Understanding how to navigate these roadblocks and work through them is crucial to helping your relationship thrive.

There are always distractions and roadblocks along the way as a couple tries to stay on the same page. Sometimes it feels like these issues are formidable. At other times, partners need to put their heads together, figure things out, and move forward together. And just like on a football team, everyone has a role to play toward the success of the relationship. When the team is struggling or trying to figure something out, charting the course together makes the process less formidable.

Rather than stepping *back* during these times, consider these periods of challenge, loss, and argument a good time to step *up*. Help your partner chart the course. Be supportive, loving, and understanding. Life happens in cycles, so it's natural for the two of you to have your ups and downs. Some days your significant other may need you to stand fast, and other days you may need them to do the same. Working together can be a powerful thing. When one of you is there to help the other, this strengthens the relationship.

One of my friends who has been married a long time jokes about how he always tries to "put money in the bank" when it comes to his relationship with his wife, meaning he takes the opportunity to do thoughtful things for her. He buys her flowers, takes her out to dinner, and tells her she looks good. He takes on tasks and gives her breaks from everyday chores. By doing these things, he's being strategic and intentional; he knows this level of attention builds goodwill in their relationship. He also realizes how his positive actions can soften the rough edges when times are not as good. During the rough patches, his kind gestures are remembered and help to keep their relationship steady and balanced.

Teamwork will always make for a better relationship, and teams can accomplish more than individuals. Teams create a stronger entity every time because when you work as a team, you have more brainpower, you have more collaboration, and you allow for the diversity of thought that leads to better solutions.

Love Check-In

For Singles:
Relationship Inventory
- If you aren't currently in a relationship, use this time to do a relationship inventory. Place two columns on a page. On the left side of the page, make note of the moments you felt your exes showed up. Write them down. On the right side of the page, note the moments you felt letdown and disappointed.

- As you reflect on this information, it will give you insights into how to communicate the ways in which you need your partner to support you physically, emotionally, financially, and perhaps spiritually. Knowing how to articulate your needs to your significant other will put you on the right path toward building a healthy relationship with them.

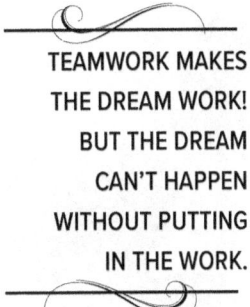

TEAMWORK MAKES THE DREAM WORK! BUT THE DREAM CAN'T HAPPEN WITHOUT PUTTING IN THE WORK.

For Couples:
Relationship-building Exercise
- Note within the next month how many times your partner shows up for you, demonstrates they care about you, and gives you gestures to show how much they love you. Reinforce this by letting them know you've noticed and are appreciative of what they're doing to nurture your relationship.
- Now do the opposite: note how many times and write down the instances when you show up for your partner and what ensues.

Teamwork makes the dream work! But the dream can't happen without putting in the work.

TEAM-BUILDING MANTRA

In my relationship, if I focus on us then we will accomplish much more.

CONCLUSION

So that's it! Remember, the five rules to a successful relationship are
1. Learn to love yourself.
2. Set realistic expectations.
3. Remember that nobody is perfect.
4. Find healthy relationships to model.
5. Make your partner your teammate.

It's up to you now to do the work required.

Relationships are not easy. That is why they are called relation-*ships*. Depending on the day, your relation*ship* can be rough sailing or steady going or somewhere in between. The key is learning to navigate, working to understand yourself and your significant other, and being able to stay the course whenever you chart rough waters.

I hope you can use the material I have provided here as you work toward the relationship you want. Repeat your mantras.

Work on your lists. Do your exercises. Investigate relationships. And remember the five rules.

Good luck!

OTHER RELATIONSHIP BOOKS TO REFERENCE

These are some of my favorite relationship resources and books I recommend to my clients.

Gary Chapman, *The 5 Love Languages: The Secret to Love that Lasts,* **Northfield Publishing, 2009.**
Dr. Chapman's book teaches readers how to keep their love tanks full by doing things that play directly to one of five love languages: Words of Affirmation, Acts of Service, Physical Touch, Quality Time, and Gifts. Since each of us has a primary love language, when you speak in someone else's love language, they are highly responsive. The book articulates why we are so responsive to partners who speak our love language.

John Gray, *Men Are From Mars, Women Are From Venus,* Harper Collins, 1992.
Dr. Gray focuses on improving the way in which men and women communicate by acknowledging these differences. He uses the analogy of Martians and Venusians who meet and have successful and happy relationships by accepting each other's differences.

Amir Levine and Rachel Heller, *Attached: The New Science of Adult Attachment and How it Can Help You Find—and Keep—Love,* TarcherPerigee, 2012.
Psychiatrist and neuroscientist Amir Levine and psychologist Rachel Heller reveal how an understanding of attachment theory focused on relationship science can help us find and sustain more long-lasting relationships. This book offers readers a wealth of advice on how to navigate their relationships more wisely given their attachment style and that of their partner. It also provides readers with a road map for building stronger and more fulfilling connections.

Phil McGraw, *Relationship Rescue: A Seven-Step Strategy for Reconnecting with Your Partner,* Hachette Books, 2001.
Dr. Phil's approach to relationships is similar to his approach to counseling. He is all about accountability, taking charge of your life, and changing yourself in order to positively change a relationship. This involves helping people to change behaviors and habits that are self-destructive. Once this occurs, people are able to diagnose, repair, and maintain their relationships.

Alicia Muñoz, *No More Fighting: 20 Minutes a Week to a Stronger Relationship*, Zephyros Press, 2018.
Conflict is inevitable in your relationship. Alicia Muñoz is a certified couples therapist who provides guidance to tackle common triggers for conflict. Alicia provides simple exercises that help readers address the fifty-two most common challenges couples face. She uses case examples and exercises that have worked for couples navigating conflict and provides a communication toolbox to help individuals maintain happy and healthy relationships.

Bessel van der Kolk, *The Body Keeps Score: Brain, Mind, and Body in the Healing of Trauma*, Penguin Publishing Group, 2015.
Bessel van der Kolk has worked with survivors of trauma for over three decades. In this book he helps us understand the impact of traumatic stress on our brain's wiring. He shows how treating significant trauma using innovative treatments, including neurofeedback, can help those who suffer from PTSD and trauma. Knowing how trauma affects the brain and body can help us understand the options available and the necessary healing measures.

ACKNOWLEDGMENTS

I have always been intrigued with dating and relationships and the dynamics that attract one person to another. As I struggled in many relationships that I thought would last a lifetime, I also observed multidecades-long marriages of so many family members: aunts, uncles, cousins, friends—people who'd found meaningful love without sacrificing their needs, confidence, or desires to do it. My parents were married for fifty-seven years. My grandparents were together for sixty-plus. These healthy love stories taught me that one was possible.

I only got to this place of understanding by studying what makes lasting love *last*. Because so often, the hardest person to see (and to love) is yourself. Yet if you could have the tools and the guide to be able to do that—to be able to love and bring your whole self into a relationship—there is a way forward to a more lasting love story. But that journey has to start with the right resources and strategies.

I learned a lot through being single, being married, coming out of a divorce, dealing with a breakup, and jumping back into the dating pool. I would like to thank my parents for their modeling of a healthy relationship, my former partners for their lessons in relationships (what to do and what not to do), and my friends and relatives for allowing me to learn about what it takes to cultivate a healthy relationship.

A special thank-you to my husband, who supported me and was extremely patient as I went through this process of writing this book. Many times when I wondered how to frame these messages to others, he was my thought partner and helped me to stay on track to ensure these messages resonated with couples to help them have happier relationships. His encouragement and steady emotional support helped me to bring this book to fruition.

Additional thanks to my sister, Rachel Overstreet; my mentors Mike and Preston; and my tribe of family and friends who are always cheering me on and encouraging me to continue to push forward. It takes a village to write a book and to deal with the periods of time a writer has to go into their isolated moments to write. I'm so fortunate to have people who understand the importance of this journey for me.

Writing this book has allowed me to share relationship learnings I have witnessed firsthand that are life changing for both couples and singles. I am excited to share with others so they don't feel like they are experiencing some of these things alone or are isolated in their relationships experiences. Thank you for allowing me to share my perspective and experiences with you too!

www.ingramcontent.com/pod-product-compliance
Lightning Source LLC
LaVergne TN
LVHW041345080426
835512LV00006B/622